Savvy Saver's EXPENSE JOURNAL

MONTHLY BILL NOTEBOOK

Activinotes

Activinotes

DAILY JOURNALS, PLANNERS, NOTEBOOKS AND OTHER BLANK BOOKS

THIS JOURNAL BELONGS TO

____

MONTH OF ______________________________

SUNDAY	MONDAY	TUESDAY	WEDNESDAY

THURSDAY	FRIDAY	SATURDAY	NOTES

THINGS TO DO

APPOINTMENTS

THINGS TO BUY

MONTH OF ______________________

SUNDAY	MONDAY	TUESDAY	WEDNESDAY

THURSDAY	FRIDAY	SATURDAY	NOTES

THINGS TO DO

APPOINTMENTS

THINGS TO BUY

MONTH OF ______________________________

SUNDAY	MONDAY	TUESDAY	WEDNESDAY

THURSDAY	FRIDAY	SATURDAY	NOTES

THINGS TO DO

APPOINTMENTS

THINGS TO BUY

MONTH OF ______________________

SUNDAY	MONDAY	TUESDAY	WEDNESDAY

THURSDAY	FRIDAY	SATURDAY	NOTES

THINGS TO DO

APPOINTMENTS

THINGS TO BUY

MONTH OF ____________________

SUNDAY	MONDAY	TUESDAY	WEDNESDAY

THURSDAY	FRIDAY	SATURDAY	NOTES

THINGS TO DO

APPOINTMENTS

THINGS TO BUY

MONTH OF ______________________________

SUNDAY	MONDAY	TUESDAY	WEDNESDAY

THURSDAY	FRIDAY	SATURDAY	NOTES

THINGS TO DO

APPOINTMENTS

THINGS TO BUY

MONTH OF ____________________

SUNDAY	MONDAY	TUESDAY	WEDNESDAY

THURSDAY	FRIDAY	SATURDAY	NOTES

THINGS TO DO

APPOINTMENTS

THINGS TO BUY

MONTH OF ____________________

SUNDAY	MONDAY	TUESDAY	WEDNESDAY

THURSDAY	FRIDAY	SATURDAY	NOTES

THINGS TO DO

APPOINTMENTS

THINGS TO BUY

MONTH OF ____________________

SUNDAY	MONDAY	TUESDAY	WEDNESDAY

THURSDAY	FRIDAY	SATURDAY	NOTES

THINGS TO DO

APPOINTMENTS

THINGS TO BUY

MONTH OF ______________________________

SUNDAY	MONDAY	TUESDAY	WEDNESDAY

THURSDAY	FRIDAY	SATURDAY	NOTES

THINGS TO DO

APPOINTMENTS

THINGS TO BUY

MONTH OF ______________________________

SUNDAY	MONDAY	TUESDAY	WEDNESDAY

THURSDAY	FRIDAY	SATURDAY	NOTES

THINGS TO DO

☐
☐
☐
☐
☐
☐
☐
☐
☐
☐
☐
☐
☐
☐
☐
☐
☐
☐
☐
☐

APPOINTMENTS

THINGS TO BUY

MONTH OF ______________________

SUNDAY	MONDAY	TUESDAY	WEDNESDAY

THURSDAY	FRIDAY	SATURDAY	NOTES

THINGS TO DO

- [ ]
- [ ]
- [ ]
- [ ]
- [ ]
- [ ]
- [ ]
- [ ]
- [ ]
- [ ]
- [ ]
- [ ]
- [ ]
- [ ]
- [ ]
- [ ]
- [ ]
- [ ]
- [ ]
- [ ]

APPOINTMENTS

THINGS TO BUY

MONTH OF ______________________________

SUNDAY	MONDAY	TUESDAY	WEDNESDAY

THURSDAY	FRIDAY	SATURDAY	NOTES

THINGS TO DO

APPOINTMENTS

THINGS TO BUY

MONTH OF ______________________________

SUNDAY	MONDAY	TUESDAY	WEDNESDAY

THURSDAY	FRIDAY	SATURDAY	NOTES

THINGS TO DO

APPOINTMENTS

THINGS TO BUY

- [ ]
- [ ]
- [ ]
- [ ]
- [ ]
- [ ]
- [ ]
- [ ]
- [ ]
- [ ]
- [ ]
- [ ]
- [ ]
- [ ]
- [ ]
- [ ]
- [ ]
- [ ]
- [ ]
- [ ]

MONTH OF ______________________________

SUNDAY	MONDAY	TUESDAY	WEDNESDAY

THURSDAY	FRIDAY	SATURDAY	NOTES

THINGS TO DO

APPOINTMENTS

THINGS TO BUY

MONTH OF ______________________________

SUNDAY	MONDAY	TUESDAY	WEDNESDAY

THURSDAY	FRIDAY	SATURDAY	NOTES

THINGS TO DO

APPOINTMENTS

THINGS TO BUY

MONTH OF ______________________________

SUNDAY	MONDAY	TUESDAY	WEDNESDAY

THURSDAY	FRIDAY	SATURDAY	NOTES

THINGS TO DO

APPOINTMENTS

THINGS TO BUY

MONTH OF ______________________________

SUNDAY	MONDAY	TUESDAY	WEDNESDAY

THURSDAY	FRIDAY	SATURDAY	NOTES

THINGS TO DO

- [ ]
- [ ]
- [ ]
- [ ]
- [ ]
- [ ]
- [ ]
- [ ]
- [ ]
- [ ]
- [ ]
- [ ]
- [ ]
- [ ]
- [ ]
- [ ]
- [ ]
- [ ]
- [ ]
- [ ]

APPOINTMENTS

THINGS TO BUY

MONTH OF ______________________

SUNDAY	MONDAY	TUESDAY	WEDNESDAY

THURSDAY	FRIDAY	SATURDAY	NOTES

THINGS TO DO

APPOINTMENTS

THINGS TO BUY

MONTH OF ______________________

SUNDAY	MONDAY	TUESDAY	WEDNESDAY

THURSDAY	FRIDAY	SATURDAY	NOTES

THINGS TO DO

APPOINTMENTS

THINGS TO BUY

MONTH OF ______________________________

SUNDAY	MONDAY	TUESDAY	WEDNESDAY

THURSDAY	FRIDAY	SATURDAY	NOTES

THINGS TO DO

APPOINTMENTS

THINGS TO BUY

MONTH OF ______________________

SUNDAY	MONDAY	TUESDAY	WEDNESDAY

THURSDAY	FRIDAY	SATURDAY	NOTES

THINGS TO DO

APPOINTMENTS

THINGS TO BUY

MONTH OF ______________________

SUNDAY	MONDAY	TUESDAY	WEDNESDAY

THURSDAY	FRIDAY	SATURDAY	NOTES

THINGS TO DO

APPOINTMENTS

THINGS TO BUY

MONTH OF ______________________________

SUNDAY	MONDAY	TUESDAY	WEDNESDAY

THURSDAY	FRIDAY	SATURDAY	NOTES

THINGS TO DO

APPOINTMENTS

THINGS TO BUY

MONTH OF ______________________________

SUNDAY	MONDAY	TUESDAY	WEDNESDAY

THURSDAY	FRIDAY	SATURDAY	NOTES

THINGS TO DO

APPOINTMENTS

THINGS TO BUY

MONTH OF ______________________

SUNDAY	MONDAY	TUESDAY	WEDNESDAY

THURSDAY	FRIDAY	SATURDAY	NOTES

www.ingramcontent.com/pod-product-compliance
Lightning Source LLC
Chambersburg PA
CBHW081336090426
42737CB00017B/3164
9781683216360